BREAKING THE INNER CHAIN

Scripture quotations are from King James Version, New Living Translation, and New King James Version, or paraphrases of these versions.

Page design: Premiere Brand
Edited by: Cassie, Gathering Leaves
Printing in the United States

Library of Congress Cataloging – in – Publication Data

ISBN-10: 0615984118
ISBN-13: 978-0615984117

Contents

Preface

Foreword

I.   Breaking The Chain of Being in the Way

II.   Breaking the Chain of an Unhealthy Lack
       of Respect for Fear

III.   Breaking the Chain of Misunderstanding

IV.   Breaking the Chain of Being Unsure of Yourself

V.   Breaking the Chain of Halted Legacy Building

VI.   Breaking the Chain of Poor Thinking

VII.   Breaking the Chain of Running Away from the Wind

VIII. Breaking the Chain of Rushing the Timing of Success

IX.   Final Thoughts

This book is dedicated to
my parents Robert & Cheryl Boyd
for their undying love for me
and raising me to understand the strength
that comes from hearing God's voice.

Breaking The Inner Chain

Pushing Through Challenges to find
the Greatness Within
YOURSELF

Malik Boyd

LIGHTHILL
PUBLISHING

FOREWORD

I heard a song sung years ago while I was in college. If the college had a billboard, this song would have been number one on the charts for weeks. The song still captures the essence of those who struggle and are held captive by chains.

When you're up against a struggle that shatters all your dreams
And your hopes have been cruelly crushed
by Satan's manifested schemes
And you feel the urge within you to submit to earthly fear
Don't let the faith you're standing in seem to disappear

Praise the Lord, He will work through those who praise Him
Praise the Lord, for our God inhabits praise
Praise the Lord, for the chains that seem to bind you
Serve only to remind you, that they drop powerless behind you
when you praise Him

Now some thirty years later, Malik Boyd has written a book that offers Twenty-First Century advice for a post modern world. His writing is easy and his admonitions of great moment today. But it is not just admonitions from an intellectual perspective, but real life stories extracted from personal experiences. I am fascinated at the way Malik skillfully weaves his experiences into this masterpiece to help those who are chained in their psyche to find freedom.

Breaking the Inner Chain provides for the reader an opportunity to start a new walk and step into a world of great possibilities. Malik Boyd has done humanity a great favor.

- Terrence D. Griffith
Senior Pastor, First African Baptist Church
President, Black Clergy of Philadelphia and Vicinity

PREFACE

Have you ever had a moment of confirmation so clear that it startled you? The kind that you became very aware that God was talking directly to you, giving you strict instructions about what to do next? Well that's what happened with me during the publishing of this book.

I am normally an "all out" kind of guy. I think of something I want to do, I commit to it, I do it. I am normally not afraid or challenged by any of the obstacles I may face.

But this book challenged me. I was very nervous about publishing it. In fact, truth be told, I had actually finished writing, submitted the manuscript to Cassie, my editor, and began to start second guessing myself.

Let's be honest here. There are many highly educated, qualified, and established individuals who could have written this book. Many of these people have multiple degrees, decades of years on the battlefield of life; they know the ropes and understand the terrain better than I. So Lord, why did you tell me to write this book? Why me?

After a few sleepless nights where I mistakenly watched Netflix in search of peace from the restlessness instead of talking to God, He brought to my remembrance a very tried but true saying, *"God doesn't call the qualified, He qualifies the called."* This saying is loosely based on a theme of the scripture verse in John 15:16, *"You have not chosen me: but I have chosen you."*

And it was this scripture that led me to this one humble request: *"God, If you have chosen me for this work, please give me a sign; confirmation that you are walking with me on this."*

My confirmation came from a sermon one Sunday shortly after. Pastor Terrence Griffith, our senior pastor, happened to be out of the country. Our guest preacher for the 11'o clock morning service was Dr. George Thornton. A very witty and socially conscious preacher, Dr. Thornton is well regarded for his ability to bring sound biblical instruction in a very relevant way. His sermon on this day just so happened to be titled *"12 Years A Slave"*. The title immediately peaked my interest, not just because of the movie from which it was inspired, but simply because I was curious where he would go with this sermon.

I can honestly tell you, the first half of his sermon, I sat on the edge of my seat, hanging to every word from the very moment he opened his mouth. The last half of his sermon, I was standing up, rocking slowly back and forth, mesmerized. At what you ask? Not by him per se, but the fact that the whole sermon was about breaking the chains of sin that stop us as individuals, as churches, and in the larger sense, a nation of Christian people from moving forward in the freedom God has designed for us. Not to mention, he kept looking at me during the sermon. But as he looked at me, I didn't see him, I saw God looking at me, confirming the mission that only a few people knew I was tasked with.

I knew at that moment, the book had to get published. And the icing on the cake was the song that was sung for invitation to discipleship:

I am free...praise the Lord, I'm free
No longer bound
No more chains holding me
My soul is resting
It's such a blessing
Praise the Lord
Hallelujah, I'm free

I realized very quickly that my fears of feeling unqualified was simply a trick for me to place myself under shackles that would confine me from sharing these stories. There were powers much greater than me working to stop this book from getting out, and accomplishing whatever God has for it to do. He called me to do this, and the only thing stopping me was the mental shackles of fear that I was ready to clamp down on my life.

For proof of how He works, let's look at the human history of God's willingness to qualify those whom He called:

Noah was a drunk.
Abraham was too old.
Isaac was a daydreamer.
Jacob was a liar.
Leah was ugly.
Joseph was abused.
Moses had a stuttering problem.
Gideon was afraid.
Samson had long hair and was a womanizer.
Rahab was a prostitute.
Jeremiah was too young.
David was an adulterer (not to mention a murderer).
Elijah was suicidal.
Isaiah preached naked.
Jonah ran from God.

Job went bankrupt.
Andrew lived in the shadow of his big brother.
Peter denied Christ.
Martha worried about everything.
The Samaritan woman was divorced (more than once).
Mary Magdalene was demon-possessed.
Zaccheus was too small.
Timothy had an ulcer.
Paul was a Christian-killer.

I am sure that all of them had felt inadequate to be chosen for the tasks God called for them to do. However, they unlocked the chains holding them back, and moved forward with God in full support.

Today, you're reading these words. The book is published. It's a clear sign that God remains victorious, and His direct will for me is non-negotiable. But it's also a sign for you. Of what you ask? That I do not know. However, I truly believe that this book was meant to be in your hands. Nothing is coincidence.

Whatever chains exist in your life, holding you back from God's promise for you, can all be broken by learning to hear God's voice in your life, committing to the directions given, and follow God's steps.

I pray that these words bless you as much as it blessed me to write them.

Lets break some chains.

Malik

BEFORE WE BEGIN

Are there any goals in your life not yet accomplished?
If so, what are they?

_____

_____

_____

_____

What are the chains in your life stopping you from accomplishing
these goals?

_____

_____

_____

_____

Are these chains mental/spiritual,/or physical?

_____

_____

_____

_____

Who has the key to these chains? Can they be removed?

_____

_____

_____

_____

Do you know what God's voice sounds like in your ear?

_____

_____

_____

_____

How does God speak to you?

_____

_____

_____

_____

I am asking you these questions now, to get honest answers from you before we dive into the chapters of this book. We will discuss these questions, and the answers you have written down, at the end of our journey.

ARE YOU READY TO BREAK SOME CHAINS?

☐ YES
(Turn page)

☐ NO
(Close book)*

* If you choose to close the book and not deal with the chains in
your life, you may literally be maling a choice to stay shackled
and stunt your progress.
(which is totally not a good look by the way)

BREAKING THE CHAIN OF BEING IN THE WAY

I

"I'm trying to make this thing happen, but these people are just in the way!"

I will never forget when I really understood this phrase. Although it was said to me in a conversation about some elected officials who were dragging their feet about getting some much-needed resources to a small community in Philadelphia, it wasn't until I took a trip to the Dominican Republic that I fully understood it.

I know you are probably thinking I'm going to tell you a story about some dramatic life-changing way I brought resources to people in need in the D.R., and I'm going to tell you that story, embellishing on my extreme amount of resolve and determination in getting the job done.

Well, I'm not.
This story is about horses.
I know, I know...
Horses.

On a recent trip to the Dominican Republic, I went out horseback riding. Having ridden a horse a few times before, I felt comfortable on the ride and enjoyed journeying through various parts of the trail, which guided our group through the white sands along the beach, in the water, and through heavily shaded areas with palm trees as a canopy.

The whole journey was a beautiful one. Getting a chance to see a little bit of the tourist areas, residents' merchant areas, and wading in water on this magnificent creature, I felt like my life at that moment couldn't get any better. I'm sure many of you have felt that way in a moment of pure tranquility.

That moment didn't stop as I dismounted and began walking to the bathrooms. As I walked in and began to wash my hands, I reinforced that feeling of tranquility with a thought...

If I could move here and live my life as a guide for visitors, riding horses all day long, I would. It would relieve me of all the stress that I deal with on a daily basis back home in the city.

That's when God poked me. Literally. Well, it really was the edge of an older model paper towel holder that had been placed extremely close to the side of the sink, but I'm sure He was responsible for it. The message He gave me right after the poke was very clear:

If you left what you do back in the United States, a career you are qualified and trained to do, to come here and work as an equestrian guide, you would be taking food out of the mouths of those who are here and need the job.

I'll be honest... Like the cartoons, a big speech bubble showed up over my head with all kinds of character symbols and marks with an exclamation point after it. You KNOW what that stood for. So did I. But so did He. And here's what He said next:

"If you left what I designed for you to do, to do what you wanted to do, you would not be doing what you were purposed to do. You're clearly not the best rider. Let's face it. And after a while, this feeling will fade. But you would dare to take the place of the man who

can do this far better than you and will treat the horses so much better than you, not because you don't love animals, but because you have no clue what it means to care for this animal or do this job."

Well, you know I wasn't feeling that. I mean, really, I desire to do it, so doesn't that count? And I am persistent and borderline compulsive on the things I want to do. Doesn't that matter? Shouldn't that actually count for something? But it really doesn't. Because at the end of the day, I may be compulsive about it, I may be persistent about it... but I don't LOVE it the way this man, who has purposed his life to become a stable keeper and guide, does. Just when I thought I had gotten all He needed to say to me, another thought dropped in:

ARE YOU LIVING THE LIFE GOD DESIGNED FOR YOU?

"The pay for what you are designed to do is far greater than the pay you desire. Even if you worked in some other country under a different pay scale, it would pale in comparison to what you can receive for doing what comes natural to you... the very thing in which I have blessed you with the gift to do."

Wow.

Now I am stuck.

Seriously.

Why are you looking at me like that?

Ok, I get it...If you don't understand what *stuck* means in this context, place any slang or jargon you prefer to use for being totally rebuked and speechless at the same time below:

_____

(write your word)

Now back to our regularly scheduled programming.

I finally got what He was trying to say to me and, through this book, what He's trying to say to you.

God gave each and every one of us something unique and special, gifts and talents that are uniquely ours. And with these gifts, we are placed on a path to make an impact in this world that only we can make. Often we do not allow our gifts to make room for us. We apply our own strategies and think that our God-given, pre-designed gifts are supposed to fit that desire. Sorry. That's not how this works.

Trying to do it your way only ensures that you will end up with roadblocks, internal challenges, feelings of inadequacy, with no solution ahead. Living within your God given design may even give you those same challenges and feelings, but the end is total-ly different. You have been prepared for that moment, with a gift designed by God that allows you to handle any issues and still come out on top.

Have you ever done what you desire to do and not what you are designed to do? How did that work out for you? For me, I can tell you it wasn't pretty. No matter how good my wonderful natural talent may have been, the things I touched and pursued that I was not designed to do just didn't work out the way they were supposed to. It was only when I surrendered to Him that everything fit into place, and the blessings soon followed.

I quickly found through all of this that some key points became very clear:

Get out of that man's room. Create your own.

The words in Proverbs 18:16 are very clear: *"A man's gift maketh room for him, and bringeth him before great men."* Your gift makes the room, not your desire. Room in your world for promotions, happiness, finances, and just about any good thing you can imagine.

Your blessings don't come from living out your desires, they come from living within your God-given design.

Psalms 34:7 says: *"Delight yourself in the Lord, and He will give you the desires of your heart."* Unless I missed something or there is some new translation I'm not aware of, one thing is certain: It is our delight in the Lord that gives us the desires of our heart. I'm sure you are wondering what does delight mean? You may be thinking, *"I do that already. I show up at church on Sunday, serve on a ministry or two. I even tithe."* But that's not what it means. Delighting ourselves in Him means to commit our daily life to Him. Doing what He designed us to do... not what we desire. He rewards us for that by giving us the very thing we desired to do in the first place, but this time without all the stress and feelings of inadequacies just an air of enjoyment... tranquility.

If we could just get out of the way of the person who can do the desired skill set better, and if we can focus on our gift—the very thing God planted in us for guaranteed success—and if we can commit our lives to living within that God-given design on a daily basis with Him as the focus... the following things are certain to be true:

- We wont be in that man's room. We'll have our own.

- We wont be in the way. We will be making ways... not only for ourselves, but for others.

- God will bless us to be able to do all the good things we desire to do, all because we were diligent about doing the very thing we were designed to do.

CHAIN BREAKERS

What unique gift and talent(s) did God give you? Do you have faith that they will make room for you?

_____

_____

_____

_____

_____

_____

Are you using those gifts/talents the way God intended, or have you allowed them to become hobbies or occasional projects?

_____

_____

_____

_____

What things can you begin to do to live by faith and begin to use these gifts/talents they way God intended?

_____

_____

_____

_____

A Penny for Your Thoughts...

Here is a section for additional notes.
Write down what you are feeling, thinking, wondering...

_____

_____

_____

_____

_____

_____

_____

_____

_____

_____

BREAKING THE CHAIN OF AN UNHEALTHY LACK OF RESPECT FOR FEAR

II

"Swimming with the sharks" has become a phrase widely used by the business community and those in politics to refer to navigating the waters with the big boys of those particular worlds. When said, it often delivers the listener an aroma of three subtle yet clear scents:

- The waters in which you dove into or navigated are dangerous.

- The sharks are predators, often kings of the environment, who are willing to view you as prey.

- You are either a shark yourself or trained in the ability to sustain yourself in their environment. Either way, you are equipped to survive.

We all have seen time and time again, from real-life scenarios to depictions on the television screen, those who have been attacked by these predators in the waters of industry and have been proven not to belong near or around that particular shark or those waters and those who have proven to survive the shark attack in their life, career, etc.

I find this correlation most fascinating. And I desire to offer you an even deeper dive, if you will, into the spiritual side of this matter.

I have a healthy respect for those who have a passion for diving, particularly those who dive with sharks. As a child, I marveled at the work of the esteemed Jacque-Yves Cousteau. I spent many hours then, even now as an adult, watching National Geographic, amazed at the divers who place themselves as a guest inside the world of sharks.

For anyone who has swum in an ocean, particularly clear waters, and has placed his or her head underwater, it immediately becomes very clear that you are a guest, not a resident. From coral reefs to schools of fish to city-size rock formations, it's quite an experience. This is a place of mystery, intrigue, and beauty. But with our human eyes only being able to see a certain distance, our ears unequipped for sonar-like hearing, and our body's design only allowing for a certain amount of swimming speed in the water, if attacked or considered prey by a creature of this silent world, the water could become dangerous, especially when a shark is involved.

Let me share with you my experience.

On one of my many passport-stamping trips out of the country (to tropical waters I might add), a very close friend of mine decided they would sign me up for swimming with stingrays and sharks. Now, quite frankly, I pride myself on being one who addresses his fear, takes it head on, and eliminates it in one fell swoop. I have always felt that if I passed away, a part of my obituary should read: *"The man who tackled and erased every fear."* To me, this experience was no different. And so I welcomed the challenge (thinly veiled as a traveler's tour gift), and I got on the boat.

(SIDE NOTE: Now for the sake of not being charged with creating pandemonium, let me note that expert studies have shown

certain kinds of sharks and certain periods of time for other sharks are not a threat. Some will even go as far as suggesting that we do more harm to sharks than they do to us. Now that I got that disclaimer out of the way... on to the rest of the story.)

As we pulled off from the dock, heading into deeper waters, I pondered over my future actions. Focusing on ensuring calm at all times, I practiced my slow breathing, worked to clear my mind, and eliminated as much angst as I could.

As we docked and anchored against the diving station, I concluded that I had effectively gone through my fear-conquering process and was fully ready to put this to bed.

The first experience was with the stingrays. Majestic creatures, they glide beautifully through the water with a ripple-like motion along the edges of their body. The particular stingray that the guide brought to me took my breath away. Almost four feet in width, I was in awe at its willingness to share its waters with me and to allow me to touch its skin. We spent time exploring the creature, the smoothness of its underbelly vs. the textured top, even watching a fellow explorer feed it sardines. I found my stingray experience most exhilarating. I was calm, at peace, and if this was any indication of what it was like to swim with sea creatures, please... I'm ready.

We got back up onto the platform and were told to begin to prepare for our experience with the sharks. My heart raced a little, but I regrouped quickly.

After placing on my mask, I jumped in the water with the guide and the others in my group and began to swim out. With a firm focus on my guide, I swam following his path. Then something clicked and I paused to take a look back at the station.

I was more than fifty feet away! Instantly my mind began to race. If something happens, I thought, I'm too far to immediately get myself right out of the water. We are all in at this point. Honestly, I'm not fond of those who act like they never have a breakdown moment or never do anything wrong or inappropriate. We are all human, and we all have our moments. Acknowledging that they exist is the first step to getting past them. So yes, there were a few other choice words that I used as well, but they would not be appropriate for this publication.

At this point, I am beginning to fear this journey. What was I thinking? Who does this and thinks this is really cool? The water visibly clear, I began to start paying attention to all of the dark spots, giant shadows casting their presence in the water. It didn't matter the shape of the spot; they were all problems to me at that point. Realizing I was on the fringes of our delegation, I also took it upon myself to carve out a space in the center of the group.

(ANOTHER SIDE NOTE: I do realize at this point in telling you my story that I have lost all ability to join the world of thug life, tough gangsters, hardcore rappers, or any group that lives and dies on showing no fear. I also am fully aware that I will not be asked to join in any videos portraying such lifestyle choices. Not that I really want to join any of those groups. I'm just acknowledging realities here. Moving on...)

Defeating my fear. I've got to do this. Fear is winning this battle. I can't let that happen. I tighten my mask and decide that I want to know exactly what these shadows...these huge, dark spots, are. Plus the guide is swimming backward and laughing. Clearly he has no worries... neither should I. I placed my body underwater and began to look down at the first dark spot. It's a large grouping of algae! Laughing to myself, I feel I am okay at this point. Plus, I'm still swimming in the middle of the group. Four more dark spots later, I decide to look down again... Still algae, but the water's getting a tad bit darker. Transitioned from a light blue to a significantly darker hue, it's harder to see what's ahead.

Then the guide starts pointing.

Yeah, I'm no longer feeling this. My heart's racing a bit more. I'm sweating in the water (a near impossible feat for the human body to achieve). Hands aren't shaking yet, but that could really go either way in about ten seconds. Still in belief that I can conquer it all, I dive under.

And that's when I see her.

Preparing to swim directly under me, bigger than the length of my body plus some, was the first of a trio of sharks. I must admit..she was gorgeous. But that didn't matter. I looked at her eyes. For the record, I'm not really sure it looked directly at me, although I really didn't care. The only thing I wanted to do was get away. And fast.

Now the account I will tell to the press is that I calmly swam in the other direction. But the real story tells a different tale. See, I was so scared of the shark that I literally breathed in with my nose... underwater. Fortunately, the scuba mask was on, so I did not take in much water. But at this point, sheer panic had sunk in. I broke the surface of the water, gasping for air, choking on the water in my lungs that was blocking the air I was gasping for, and now recognizing that I was in trouble. The interesting thing about it; nothing was attacking me! I did it to myself. The first lesson of swimming with sharks: Make sure that you can really handle the presence of a shark before you get in the water, let alone decide to swim with a group of them.

If you remember, in the beginning of my encounter with the first shark, I told you that it was the first of three. That means in the midst of my choking, gasping, praying, etc., there were still two more sharks that I had probably just alerted.

Despite my apparent requests to see God quicker than He intended, I stuck my head back under to see what was happening. The other two sharks were just passing under me, swimming in close proximity to each other almost as if their fins were high-fiving each other. I don't speak shark, but I believe they were probably laughing at the way they just punked the 6'4" black man.

I thought to myself, I have clearly failed this mission, but the worst is over. Actually, it wasn't.

There was a fourth shark, in the distance, decisively bigger than the others, and he was headed our way. He wasn't really concerned with us, more curious than anything, but that did not subside the intense fear building up inside of me. So what did I do? Funny you should ask. I immediately turned my back. Why? Well in my mind, I figured, *Hey… if I have to go, I'll go with him biting me on the behind. I definitely don't want to watch this go down.*

I'm still speaking to you now so its clear he didn't take me out. He didn't brush up against me. I don't even think he paid attention to me. When I thought the coast was clear and looked past my feet, he was far off in the water. Needless to say, I made a beeline back to the station, Michael Phelps style. I hopped up on the deck, threw off the mask, and jumped right onto the boat. To me, not even the planks of the station were safe.

So… here I am, standing literally in the middle of the boat. And that's when He started speaking to me. That's right, God started speaking to me right at that moment.

He said, *"Go back and look in the water."* I went and looked. *"Tell me, what do you see?"*

People swimming, I noted sarcastically. He said, *"Look closer."*

As I looked the second time, I saw some people actually following the sharks around. They were swimming on the surface, but they were doing the very thing our guide asked them not to do: trying to provoke the shark with big movements and heavy splashing. The next thing I saw were two people who were clearly in panic mode, similar to the state in which I had found myself. They didn't think to jump out of the water. They were clinging safely to the back of the guide. The next thing I saw was the third guide. He was in the water but looking at me, waving, with a smile on his face. Even though I left his side to go back, he wasn't laughing at me. He was waving to make sure I was okay.

Then I got it.

My swimming excursion is very similar to life. In the waters of our lives, sharks are everywhere, spiritually intimidating us, trying to make us drown, and placing fear in our ability to maneuver comfortably in the water.

Spiritual energy entered the world and covered it the moment Adam and Eve decided to sin before God. Adam's imputed sin, often refered to as the *orinigal sin*, served as a turn of the handle on a faucet, ensuring that sin would ultimately cover the earth. Like the waters covering the deep, so too did the spiritual energy rise and began to cover the earth. We found ourselves spiritually underwater, swimming with sharks. Even though we are all creatures, our design as humans doesn't allow us to swim in these waters without help. We need air to stay underwater, we need fins to try to enhance our speed and maneuverability, we need diver suits to protect our skin, and we need a guide... simply because we don't know our way.

Scripture is clear: *"For we wrestle not against flesh and blood but against principalities, wickedness in high places."* This refers to those spiritual sharks we swim with. They are not human beings. They have fins, rows of teeth, and the capability to catch us at any time if they wanted to engage us. As humans, because we are not designed to swim in these waters, we are viewed as the prey. This is their home. And our safety lies in our ability to stay alert, stay calm, and follow the instructions of the guide.

The three actions we can learn from this are as follows:

Stay Alert.

The first key to releasing fear is being alert. Yes, you could argue that I was alert to some extent during my time in the water. After all, I watched every dark spot that I could see. But that was when my head was above the water, looking down. In order to see the spiritual sharks clearly, you need to get your head in the water, spiritually becoming aware of your surroundings and being able to clearly distinguish what is a threat to your energy and well-being and what is not.

Stay Calm.

The 23rd Psalm is one of the most widely recited Bible passages of today's time. We often find it utilized in teaching our young children how to pray before bed. But in the context of this conversation, and many other times, it is also utilized as the prayer many say when in the face of grave danger.

The challenge found with most that say this prayer in the midst of danger is the fact that it is said with fear. This fear, normally dressed with an outfit of a clear lack of calm, actually defeats the purpose of the prayer, contradicting its very words. We breeze through the prayer, missing the impact of the first line: *"The Lord is my Shepard, I shall not want."* – Psalm 23:1

Well, if he is our Shepard, a protector, one who has more ability to defend us than we ourselves, what is there that we could actually want? The matter is settled right in that first powerful declaration.

But by chance you miss that line, there is another one that is very clear and direct:

"Yea though I walk through the valley of the shadow of death, I will fear no evil." – Psalm 23:4

Does it get any more specific than that? Shadows… Remember how I described the black areas in the water? There is no need, no reason to fear anything evil or negative energy. The shadows of death have no effect when I am calm in the presence of my guide.

Which leads me to my last point.

Follow The Guide.

Those who are destined to find themselves in trouble, ultimately being forced to choose between a fight or flight position, with panic coursing through their veins, are often those who have a problem listening to instructions. The guide is there for a reason... They know the territory! They understand the waters in which you are exploring for your first time. In some cases, they are even familiar with the huge creatures you will face.

Like the swimmers I saw from the boat, splashing in the water, provoking the sharks, we too can find ourselves placing ourselves at risk of becoming a target when we don't follow the rules of the road. The guide has those rules in the water. Our spiritual guide, the word of God, has those rules for our spiritual waters. And for those who cannot clearly hear the voice of the guide in their life, they should hold on to the Word—literally —as the two swimmers did on my excursion.

Don't be like me. Don't run for the station first chance you get. If you do, you never get a chance to finish the experience because you have left the water. In my case, fear won.

So stay alert, stay calm, and follow your guide. If you do, you can lose your fear for good and make the best of your experience of life.

CHAIN BREAKERS

In your life, do you find yourself "swimming with sharks"? If so, have you clearly identified them, and know where you encounter them?

_____

_____

_____

_____

_____

_____

How do you act when you find yourself in these waters? Are you calm when you encounter these "sharks" or do your actions show fear?

_____

_____

_____

_____

Have you clearly identified the guide who God has placed in the water to help you navigate your "shark" experience?

_____

_____

_____

_____

Read the 23rd Psalms. Give some thought to the author's words. How do you think he really felt as he penned those words? How could he be so sure that God had his back in the midst of trouble?

_____

_____

_____

_____

How has God proven to have your back during rough times? Can you think of any "swimming with shark" moments that God already guided you successfully through?

_____

_____

_____

A Penny for Your Thoughts...

Here is a section for additional notes.
Write down what you are feeling, thinking, wondering...

_____

_____

_____

_____

_____

_____

_____

_____

_____

_____

_____

_____

_____

_____

_____

_____

_____

_____

_____

BREAKING THE CHAIN OF MISUNDERSTANDING

III

In living this life the few days that I have been blessed to live, I have fully subscribed to the thought that many of the misunderstandings and challenges that we have surrounding our success do not come from external factors, but from simply not having a clear understanding of who we really are. Life, just like the movies, has afforded us a leading role. It is our job to stay in character.

Let's ponder this for a second... As a director of a film, could you imagine working on a set with an actor who simply could not stay in character? It would be the most frustrating thing, trying to film scenes, you're dealing with time constraints, and you have a rogue actor. That jeopardizes the whole film. Now get this... Here's what's even worse: having the lead actor not only refuse to say the lines designed for them, but start reciting the lines of one of the extras!

Does that make sense to you?

I didn't think so. I mean, really, I would be seriously confused, disappointed, or frustrated if I went to the movies to see Will Smith in Ali and he decided he was only going to play the role of the one of the villagers in Manila.

In life, however, we find ourselves impeding our positive impact and stunting our success by doing the same thing. Although we are designed to play this leading role in life, we decide that we are going to play a supporting role or even the role of the extras. Some rationalize this choice by suggesting things like, *"Being the lead guy has too much drama around it,"* or, *"I just want to get in, do what I have to do, and go home. Don't need anything extra."* Have you allowed any of those kinds of statements to come from your lips? Or maybe there is another phrase you like to say. Either way, allow me to humbly place something before you in response.

You are a descendant from a line of royalty. No. Seriously. You are. A chosen people, a royal priesthood, to be exact. In fact, those are the words Jesus used to describe you.

"But ye are a chosen generation, a royal priesthood, an holy nation, a peculiar people; that ye should shew forth the praises of him who hath called you out of darkness into his marvelous light;"
- 1 Peter 2:9

So the reality is that you were designed for this. You were created to be someone special. The very energy flowing inside of you comes from a higher power whose sole purpose in granting you this power was so you could continue the greatness of the lineage. Rightfully make your mark in the family tree.

Because of this lineage that you are a part of, there are some things that are written just for you.

After all, God's movie called *Life* was written with you as the star. Now I'm sure you are wondering, *Well, if I am the star of my life, if I am truly royalty, why does everything around me look like hell? Why am I challenged on every turn with difficulty and turmoil? And where's my green room? Where's my catered lunch?* I truly understand. I get it. Let me answer clearly.

If you are asking yourself the questions above, it's possible that you misunderstood what comes with being who you are. First, please understand this:

To whom much is given, much is required.

That isn't just some cute line to be used when we want to sound sophisticated, mature, and full of wise counsel. It's truth. Yes, royalty comes with a lot of sexy stuff. But it also comes with some major responsibility. In your greatness, you will be required to handle more than what you are used to. The greatest rulers—those who are good enough to stay on top—understand that there is a lot of work that goes into getting there and staying there. Have you ever considered that those who exhibit impactful leadership and have staff/teams that are loyal to no end often feed their staff/team first, before they eat? As leaders, they are willing to go without so that others around them can benefit. And they do so without complaining while they take care of their team.

Let's face it... To be successful at life, you need a team that you can count on. But that reliability is birthed from your team's ability to count on you; to count on you being able to go the extra mile, and working harder than them. It is this characteristic of leadership that will take all of you to the next level. There is no leader that can work by themselves and have defined, lasting success. Even Jesus had disciples.

Secondly, I implore you to think about this:

Royalty/leadership that lasts does so because those in position learn that it's all about service, not sitting.

Think about this:

- Medieval kings would consider it an honor to lead their knights in battle.

- No one respects or wants to vote for the politician who is never in the community, doing the work.

- Martin Luther King, Jr. would not have had the same level of impact if he tried to manage his participation in the Civil Rights Movement from an office and never marched with the people. Who's going to stand firm in protest and keep taking water hoses to the face if the leader, the one who has all the mouth, won't do it?

And this service that I speak of—the service that makes a positive, lasting impact—often requires you to leave the comfort of the throne (i.e. your comfort zone) and step out into the unknown, all the while keeping the same level of excellence that you would have on your throne (your comfort zone).

Which leads me to my third point: **Breaking out of your comfort zone with a spirit of service not only blesses others, but also blesses you.**

CHAIN BREAKERS

What do you think it takes to be a leader? Are you up to the task of leading others?

_____

_____

_____

_____

What are the areas/situations/scenarios in your life in which you can take a leadership role?

_____

_____

_____

_____

_____

Now that you know what areas you can impact by leading, ask yourself this serious question: Are you identifying these areas as possible opportunities to serve or simply be seen?
(answer honestly)

_____

_____

_____

_____

_____

Identify a Leader in your community / network. Who are they? Why do you consider them a leader? List the traits they exhibit that you admire. Consider asking them to serve as your mentor.

_____

_____

_____

_____

_____

_____

_____

_____

A Penny for Your Thoughts...

Here is a section for additional notes.
Write down what you are feeling, thinking, wondering...

_____

_____

_____

_____

_____

_____

_____

_____

_____

_____

_____

_____

_____

_____

_____

_____

_____

_____

_____

BREAKING THE CHAIN OF BEING UNSURE OF YOURSELF

IV

I love the movie Coming To America. I truly believe it was one of the most classic performances by Eddie Murphy and Arsenio Hall. Why I love this movie, however, is not just for the acting, but also for the lessons that emanate from the storyline. If by chance you have not seen the movie, let me give you a brief synopsis.

Eddie Murphy plays Akeem, this young prince who is heir to the throne of a country named Zumunda. He decides to bring his desires to his father, who is reluctant but agrees at the persistence of his mother to allow him to travel to New York of all places to... sow his royal oats.

They journey to New York, marveling at the wow factor of the city. This place, this city has grit... an edge to it that is unfamiliar to Eddie. But he insists on taking an apartment of low stature in order to assimilate to the current culture he sees.

Now Arsenio's character, Simi, is not happy about this, but after a few failed attempts to get Eddie to give up the pauper lifestyle and upgrade, he relents.

During this journey, Akeem meets a young woman he is head over heels for. This would be a perfect scenario for him, except she is in a relationship with a guy named Darryl, the heir to a hair care company fortune, and well... her father is 150 percent in support of Darryl.

Most facing that level of opposition would tend to go toe-to-toe with Darryl and his hair care fortune. After all, Akeem is a prince with a country's worth of riches. But instead, he decides to go to work for McDowell's, a fictional spin-off of McDonald's. This food venue happens to be owned by the father of Akeem's love interest.

Now for a prince, this seems like work beneath Akeem. Simi, his friend, certainly felt so! So why would Prince Akeem, someone with access to a vast amount of wealth and resources at his beckon call, allow himself to be ridiculed by Darryl?

Why would Akeem be willing to go work at a place of meager earnings, placing himself far below the high-level social scale that his competition operated on? Why wouldn't Akeem choose to use his wealth and status to change his current outlook or influence the outcome of his quest? It seems clear that Akeem understood the following truths that we can utilize in our daily lives:

Believe it or not, your obstacles are more scared of you than you are of them.

Darryl, the boyfriend and heir to the hair care company throne, spent a considerable amount of his time trying to deflate Akeem, from making fun of his heritage, his attire, and his personality to mocking him openly in front of others and his love interest. The funny thing about all of it is that Darryl exhibited behavior that showed not only blind arrogance, but fear as the movie progressed. He became aware that there was something special about this guy Akeem and he was a threat that needed to be neutralized. That's what the impact of your royalty does... It creates fear in the heart of your obstacles. Because they can try all they want to damage you, but they cannot take away your impact.

Why? Because your power, your energy is not an external force...
It is an internal force with an external impact.

The key to your ability to stand tall comes from knowing WHO and WHOSE you are.

Akeem knew he was a prince. He understood that the riches his family had amassed were far greater than anything Darryl could present to the love interest. That gave him the ability to be calm and collected under pressure because he was absolutely sure of his value. Have faith in who and whose you are. You are the child of the King, heir to the riches of a vast kingdom. This makes you quite the valued individual. You are not what you thought you were. You are so much more.

DO YOU REALLY KNOW HOW RICH YOU ARE?

Knowing your value and understanding how much you are worth enables you to evaluate the scenario before you with a clear head, because you are no longer trying to assess or prove your worth, but now determine which exchanges or interactions are worth your time and energy.

The God in you is bigger than the problem around you.

Sure, many of you will wonder why I am still using Coming to America as a reference when it comes to making this point. It's true; the movie does not have much to do with church or anything spiritual. However, those who choose to embrace that thought will miss the point. Because of the knowledge that Prince Akeem had of himself, he was able to walk with integrity, serve/work with humility, yet exude a strong dedication to excellence. His willingness to choose modesty over flashy exuberance, and to suppress his desire to showcase his wealth, yet use it to bless others *(the generous offering scene at the talent show and the bag of money to Mortimer and Randolph, the homeless men)* are all character traits of a man who is truly grounded spiritually and understands his purpose.

It was those character traits that won over Akeem's love interest, not his money. So if these things are true and indeed factual, then it is safe to say:

- When you know your obstacles are afraid of you…

- When you know who you are and whose you are…

- When you know that the God-like character traits you exhibit have more impact on your challenges than your challenges have on you…

Then you can stand in the midst of anything and be totally sure of not only yourself, but also your capabilities, and you can deliver top-peak performance in whatever you are called to do because there is truly nothing to fear. **Who you are and who lives inside of you is greater than anything you face.**

CHAIN BREAKERS

Who are you? What do you represent? Who do you represent?

_____

_____

_____

_____

In your last answer, did you define yourself by your career, your academic status, or material things? Or did you talk about your God given value? If so, why?

_____

_____

_____

_____

What obstacles in your life can be overcome simply by your understanding and expression of your God-given royal status?

_____

_____

_____

_____

A Penny for Your Thoughts...

Here is a section for additional notes.
Write down what you are feeling, thinking, wondering...

_____

_____

_____

_____

_____

_____

_____

_____

_____

_____

_____

_____

_____

_____

_____

_____

_____

_____

_____

_____

BREAKING THE CHAIN OF HALTED LEGACY BUILDING

V

"We are all interconnected by an inescapable chain of mutuality…"

—Dr. Martin Luther King, Jr.

This chapter is truly an emotional one. It may spark some formerly buried feelings, memories, or issues previously not dealt with within your life. For this I apologize, but these moments are needed to get this point across.

We face an ever-changing landscape. Technology is creating as many challenges as opportunities; media messages are focused on self-preservation within the corporate workplace. We even find ourselves glued to the television during prime time to view political shows that fuel the message of cutting the career throats of others in order to maintain our own ability to swallow.

We purchase self-help books, ballooning the bottom line of publishers and bookstores everywhere, finding new ways to strengthen our positions in life. And I will be the first to say that these books have merit. However, in the midst of all of this focus on self, we miss the biggest opportunity of all: the ability to secure our legacy, not by miraculous feats of accomplishment married to self-promotion, but simply by helping each other.

I know… You're going to tell me how many charities you donate to and how many people you feed at Thanksgiving. You will bring up the point that you have adopted a child in a other country through some not-for-profit organization. But that's not what I am referring to. I'm talking about making a lasting impact through your ability to impact the next generation of leaders.

It's true, we can make some dent in the nation's issues by donating to charities on a monthly basis. The truth is our donations are often so segmented by cause, location, non-profit, etc., that we truly don't close the deal on many of the issues we donate to. But that is not today's challenge, tomorrow's problem.

Today's challenge is the fact that in many parts of our country, our next generation lacks mentorship. They lack an opportunity to know that someone outside of their parents has a vested interest in them and is willing to stand by them and see them to the platform of success.

You could complain that they don't want to listen or that they are walking around with a chip on their shoulder. But have you ever stopped to ask yourself why? None of the next generation I have ever met has told me that they wished to be here... that they emailed their parents or sent an inbox on social media asking for a delivery date. They entered the world in the midst of what we know now to be the end of a financial boom, but also a deficit of true love within the families. Many were conceived with a parent present but had to grow up with him absent. They are told that jobs await them if they get a good education, but they watch adults fight politically over money that should be there to secure a quality education. They get an education, only to find that the job market is dried up because of choices made by the previous generation. They learn that the rising of the U.S. debt ceiling is really the indicator of how much debt is on their heads the moment they are able to pay taxes. They search to find out how much of that debt ceiling is allocated to truly help them innovate industries and generate more income but find out there is not much on the political line item budgets to move the dial toward them. Add a few youthful mistakes along the way and you have a recipe for challenges to last through the ages.

Yes, the problems they face are very real. And quite frankly, some of what they face is by actions of their own choosing. But isn't that the same thing we experienced as youth? Didn't we make mistakes also? Didn't someone step in and lend you a hand and lift you up?

MENTORSHIP IS OUR OBLIGATION NOT AN OPTION.

Most men who've experienced an urban setting during their rearing affectionately give that person the title *"my oldhead."* And while your *"oldhead"* imparted wisdom into your being and pushed you along the path, the reality is that they were building their own legacy by giving you the tools and the "know how" to create your own.

If by chance you are one of the superhero few that made it on your own with no mentorship, with no one spending time to impart jewels of wisdom in your world, then I salute you and implore you to skip this chapter. The rest of us will join you later.

Now for those of us who have come to the point of acceptance, we acknowledge that we have some level of wisdom imparted to us by those who have gone before that enables us to move with confidence in this world. We also come to the conclusion that we are old enough to plant seeds of our own. This is our obligation, not our option. Yes, it is easy to be selfish. It is easy to think of only your family and no one else. You've survived hell and high water to get here. Why should you have to share in the spoils with others? You have to because that is the true gift of life. You receive purely because you give purely. We do not live in a vacuum. You are not solo on this island. If we do not come together, share the burden and the blessing as a collective, we are doomed to fail.

FIND PERSONAL HEALING BY BECOMING A MENTOR.

I know the world has kicked you when you were down.

I know Dad wasn't there.

I know you have worked hard for every penny that has come in your home.

I know you have shed tears behind closed doors.

I know some of you have become so hardened by life that you can't cry anymore, even when you want to.

I know you still dream but wonder how you can ever accomplish them with the realities you face now.

I know you've had pressure all your life to be perfect, and at this point you feel like you're ready to crack.

I know you are still dealing with issues of being abused as a youth.

I know you have fought for years to be hardcore and difficult because you weren't shown much love growing up.

I know that abandonment you experienced in your yesterdays affects many of the decisions you make in your todays.

I know it's still hard to show love now.

I know in your current or past relationships you may have experienced challenges of commitment, because no one ever showed commitment to you.

I get it. Trust me, I do. But now is where it all changes.

How?

By helping another young person deal with life's issues and heal from their wounds.

"Why should I?" you ask. Because in helping another heal, you heal yourself. By imparting the wisdom, pain, and realities of experience into our young people, you:

- Give the real sense of what the world really is.

- Reduce the naiveté and increase the awareness.

- Ensure your legacy by placing your wisdom in the heart of one who will carry it long after you're gone.

- Increase your karma and goodwill by showing that you care about more than yourself and your immediate family.

- In some cases, the young person you impact by legacy building ends up the very person prepared to carry your work forward.

- Increase the chances of success for that young person and help the economy sustain itself during your time of retirement.

- Blessings begin to come in ways that you never thought because the seeds you planted began to take root and grow fruit.

What we must remember is that in our generation, none of us made it on our own. And when we recognize it, we understand that we can't demand from the next generation while leaving them on their own. It's impossible; it's failure in the making. Not only for the economy, for our own legacies, but also for the moral stability of our community.

Many of us argue that the next generation doesn't respect what we have done or accomplished. But why should they? Have you spent time talking to them about how it was done, or what it cost to accomplish the task? Or did you tell them how you failed before you achieved success? Frankly, our *"oldheads"* said the same about us. So... how do we make a difference? How do we help to change the landscape and build a strong future? How do we ensure that our stories of accomplishments and triumph are told for years to come? Consider doing these things:

- Mentor a young man or woman. The time spent will change their life and yours.

- Don't take the easy way out and mentor someone who is clearly already on his or her way. Find someone to mentor who really needs your presence.

- Share your knowledge. Training the next generation to be better than you does not threaten your job security; it only increases your legacy.

- Doing nothing to help the next generation during a crisis hurts just as much as intentionally harming them.

- Always remember, whether intentional or unintentional, cutting the throat of the next generation only restricts your ability to swallow.

The next generation is our future. They are the carriers of the scrolls of history. Some day, they will open them up and read them line-by-line. Make sure your name is there. Ensure your legacy is read tomorrow by pouring into them today.

CHAIN BREAKERS

When you watch the news, and hear the reports of some of the devious actions of our young people, do you get angry at them or does your heart ache for them? Why?

_____

_____

_____

_____

If you are willing, identify and write down a child (not your own), that you can mentor. Why did you choose this young person?

_____

_____

_____

_____

_____

_____

What is your legacy? What will you teach him/her?

_____

_____

_____

_____

_____

_____

A Penny for Your Thoughts...

Here is a section for additional notes.
Write down what you are feeling, thinking, wondering...

_____

_____

_____

_____

_____

_____

_____

_____

_____

_____

_____

_____

_____

_____

BREAKING THE CHAIN OF POOR THINKING

VI

Poor thinking hinders your success. Period. I could stop there, but then I would have to explain why this chapter is so short. I'm not really sure there is a good enough PR spin to accomplish that. Therefore, I'm going to flush this principle out through the following trains of thought.

Success requires you to stop thinking poorly. And no, I'm not talking dollars and cents, per se; however, the way you think does affect your dollars and cents.

Many a barber shop or beauty salon has been filled with conversation from people surrounding feelings of being held back at work, overlooked, feelings that suggest that greatness is not in the plan for their life. For some, poor thinking ends up in language that sounds like, *"I'm just tired of 'The Man' holding me back."* (I've never met The Man by the way).

Some are even bold enough to say, *"God has me right here in this place. And I'm just gonna live out this season of my life."* (That may be true, but it normally doesn't apply to the scenario at the time). You may even hear things like, *"There's just too much politics in my job. I can't get past it."* I would argue that politics are not the issue... It's personalities. Politics becomes a good blanket word to address the issue as a whole. But the reality is you are dealing with the personality of the co-worker, manager, or boss... and therein lies the problem. So with that said, let's dig in.

Never get caught up staying in your lane.

In the course of your life, at some point, you had the opportunity to travel a road. Whether by car, bus, truck, or motorcycle, you had the opportunity to interact with other drivers while traveling to your destination.

The truth of the matter is there is not one of you who hasn't changed lanes at some point in order to either evade an obstacle in the road or take an opportunity to get further in the pack than where you currently are.

In fact, there are a few of us on this planet that suffer from a condition known as road rage. Road rage tends to develop when someone is in your lane, hindering your ability to move forward (quickly, in most cases), and/or creating a hazard that could end up in one or both of you getting injured by crashing. While most of us who experience road rage also exhibit some interesting behavior and can be found coloring our vocabulary and gesturing as we change lanes and move around, the point is we change lanes. We move around the obstacle.

If we are willing to change lanes as we drive our cars, why do we find ourselves so fearful of changing lanes on the road of life? People will tell you all the time, *"Stay in your lane."* Why? If there is an obstacle in front of me or if the cars ahead are moving at a snail's pace, I'm not waiting for them to decide to speed up to my pace... I'm going around.

So many of us wonder why the promotion we desire so badly is taking years to get. Change lanes. Stop coming to work, doing things only to just get by. Take some initiative, rev your output engine, and show that you have the ability to turn up the pace.

We wonder why our progress in our personal relationships seems to have a bland feel to it. It could be that you are cruising in pack of *"Sunday drivers,"* those who are driving with no concernabout anyone else's pace. They are content with taking every ounce of their sweet time, snail pacing down the road, ultimately slowing you up in the process. Change lanes. Throw on your signal, check your mirrors, and move! Put some horse-power in the relationship by putting more of your energy into moving the relationship   forward. Change the perspective for you and your significant other. The lane you are in on many roads makes a differ-ence in what you and your passenger get a chance to see through the win-dow.

CHANGING LANES CAN POSITIVELY CHANGE YOUR LIFE.

And trust me, on the road of life, your personal relationship may find you on the road of life during some *"Monday morning"* traffic. The road is crowded, everyone driving is frustrated, and the time is becoming more precious by the minute. Being willing to change lanes is not just a good option, but necessary if you ever plan to get any-where. And if you and your significant other are wise enough to keep God in your life, that makes three of you in the car, and you can take the carpool lane, which almost always allows you to simply whiz by all the commotion. (Now *that's* a sermon for another day.)

Now some of you are still not convinced. All your life you have been conditioned to believe that staying in your lane is a sure way to be a team member, not create disruption, and be produc-tive. Not so much. That's called playing your position. Staying in your lane and playing your position are two different things.

Staying in your lane can actually impede your progress. Playing your position will enhance your progress and positively impact others. Playing your position is focused around making the best and broadest impact you can through the circumstance in which you find yourself. For example, if your life currently has you driving the *"career car"* of account executive, no matter what lane (company) you are in, no matter the current pace in which you determine to drive, be the best account executive you can be.

Play your position by working those accounts, serving your clients with excellence, and showing integrity through your interactions.

Good drivers simply drive well. Outside of following rules of the road, they know how to drive in a way that doesn't impede others and perform on the road in a way that makes it easier for people to share the road with them. After all, as drivers, we tend not to care about the other drivers that change lanes when they are willing to throw on a signal or courteous enough to ask to get over. The same is true on the road of life.

Great endings have humble beginnings.

Michael Jordan is arguably the best player to ever play basketball. His accolades and accomplishments read like the resume of a true superhero: Six NBA Championships, six NBA Finals MVP awards, five NBA MVP awards, ten NBA scoring titles, fourteen NBA All Star selections, three NBA All-Star MVP selections, eleven All NBA selections, and nine Defensive First Team selections. What's amazing about it is with everything listed above it only amounts to roughly thirty percent of his accomplishments!

Michael's performance on the court was one of legend. One of his most defining performances was on June 14, 1998, game six of the NBA Finals against the Utah Jazz.

The Bulls were ready to clinch the series. They had missed the chance to do it in Chicago and found themselves locked into a battle in Utah. Now the truth is Jordan wasn't at his best during this game. He had only completed nine of his twenty-five shots in the previous game. But tonight would not only make up for that mild temperature performance; it would define a career.

It was deep in the fourth quarter, less than one minute on the clock. The Bulls were trailing by one, 86-85. Utah had possession of the ball. In true superhero form, Jordan stripped the ball from Karl Malone, an amazing power forward built like a prototype warrior, who was nicknamed *"The Mailman"* for his ability to deliver in clutch moments. Jordan pushed the ball down court. He saw Steve Kerr on the wing, guarded by Utah's all-star guard John Stockton.

Jordan knew in his mind that Stockton couldn't leave Kerr to help on defense. That reality left Jordan alone for a classic one-on-one with Utah's Byron Russell. Just inside the three-point line, Jordan began his move. He stutter-stepped, pushing the ball on the floor with a crossover dribble. Russell made the fatal flaw of reaching for the ball. The moment he did, Jordan made his move, locking Russell into an awkward off-balance pose that ultimately ended up with him on the floor as Jordan rose to take the jump shot, perfectly centered at the top of the key. With his arm extended, Jordan stood at the top of the key as he, along with seemingly the whole world, watched the ball drop perfectly through the net. The buzzer sounded, and the Bulls solidified another championship with an 87-86 win.

Here's what I love about that game. It wasn't his performance. I mean surely the shot was incredible, but there was more of a message in this than the winning shot. It was the fact that his most significant moment wasn't defined by the final action; it was defined by the work and events leading up to the shot.

See, no matter what championship game we are talking about, no matter how great the ending result, it all started from a simple "tip off."

I'm going to show you in one of my favorite cadence styles why all of this matters. Now let's trail Jordan's final shot as a Bull back to his "tip off" moment.

Jordan made the final shot in game six of the 1998 NBA Finals against the Utah Jazz.

That final shot would have never been made if Jordan didn't steal the ball from Karl Malone.

He could have never stolen the ball from Karl Malone if Jordan wasn't in the game, playing for Chicago against Utah.

The game between Chicago and Utah would not have occurred if Jordan had not performed at the level he did during the 1998 season.

Jordan would have never performed at the level he did during the 1998 season if he didn't spend the time working hard during the offseason with the Bulls team.

Jordan would have never had an offseason to practice with Bulls team members if the Chicago Bulls had not drafted him.

The Chicago Bulls would not have drafted Jordan if he had not performed at a high level in college at North Carolina.

Jordan would not have performed well in North Carolina if Coach Dean Smith had not believed in his ability and placed him in a key position. Dean Smith would not have placed Jordan in a key position on the North Carolina team if Jordan didn't show the work ethic it took to be a star player at the college level.

Jordan would not have shown the work ethic it took to be a star player at the college level if it wasn't for his great performance in high school varsity level at Emsley A. Laney High School.

Jordan would have never had the great performance for the Emsley A. Laney High School varsity basketball team if it weren't for Coach "Pop" Herring placing him on the JV basketball team.

Jordan would have never been placed on the JV basketball team if it weren't for his tremendous work ethic.

Jordan would have never had the tremendous work ethic if it wasn't for his good friend Harvest Leroy Smith, being taller than Jordan at the time, making the varsity team and pushing Jordan to practice harder.

Jordan would have never met Harvest Leroy Smith and been pushed to practice harder if it wasn't for his father placing a court in the backyard of the house.

So you can see, just from the small trail of breadcrumbs present-ed before you, it's clear that Michael's great moment of 1998 in Utah really came from a very humble beginning in Wilmington, North Carolina. That was really the "tip off."

Pause for a second. Can you trace the trail of events back to your "tip off" moment? Can you visualize the path to greatness and the steps that have, in their sequential impact, prepared you for what's ahead?

I encourage you to stop looking at one simple moment in time as the only possibility for definition of your greatness. Your greatness began the moment you were born. In fact, while you were still in the womb, your greatness was being prepared and prepped for definition. The moment your mother gave birth to you, you were also impregnated with greatness. It's the steps you take next, the responses you have to environmental factors, and the desire to achieve success that determine the moment of birth for your greatness.

Thinking in "stages and steps" is vital to seeing your vision through.

I have yet in this life seen a caterpillar immediately sprout wings, change shape, just decide to become a butterfly. I have yet to see a five-year-old become a professor of a university. Nor have I seen a seed grow immediately into a tree. (No beanstalks over here, Jack).

My point is this… Everything happens in time. And when you rush the time, you place the very thing you are trying to build in danger. Trying to pull a caterpillar out of a cocoon while in trans-formation places it at risk. Placing a five-year-old as a professor at a university would not only place the child in a position of not being able to deliver, thus setting he or she up for failure, but also placing the enrolled college-level students at a disadvantage by having a professor grossly under-prepared to properly instruct. Nothing good comes out of moving any of these scenarios forward before the subject is ready and the time is at hand.

All matters of life are the same way. Your greatness will come. Your success will come. Your transformation will come... all in due time. Understand your purpose in this life (which is directly connected to your greatness); plan according to the stages and steps that ensure proper development. You cannot properly "change lanes" unless you first learn how to drive.

CHAIN BREAKERS

What is your humble beginning? Can you trace back to your "tip off" moment?

_____

_____

_____

_____

_____

_____

Have you found yourself "staying in your lane", never changing lanes, allowing the car of another's life in front of you to dictate your life's progress? If so, why?

_____

_____

_____

_____

_____

_____

What are the steps and stages needed to successfully change lanes and move forward in your life?

_____

_____

_____

_____

_____

_____

_____

_____

_____

_____

_____

Who travels with you in the car of your life? Do you find yourself picking up "hitch hikers"?

_____

_____

_____

_____

_____

_____

A Penny for Your Thoughts...

Here is a section for additional notes.
Write down what you are feeling, thinking, wondering...

_____

_____

_____

_____

_____

_____

_____

_____

_____

_____

_____

_____

_____

_____

_____

_____

_____

_____

_____

BREAKING THE CHAIN OF RUNNING AWAY FROM THE WIND

VII

Learning how to fly a plane is one of my most exciting and amazing experiences. Hands down. Yes, diving off cliffs is cool, driving a race car at a private camp might bring a thrill, but there is absolutely nothing more amazing to me than the feeling of achieving "wheels up." That is the moment you are lifting up off the ground and taking off into the "wild blue yonder."

I'll never forget my first lesson… in a small but friendly airport in Northeast Philadelphia, with a young man not more than twenty -six years of age. He was 5'6", chiseled facial features, small wiry frame, very deeply confident in his flying ability. I admit, I was initially envious of his youth and his five-plus years of flying, wishing that I too had started this journey earlier in my life. After some small talk and getting my ground instructions, we headed out the door for our walk to the hangar.

Now this day happened to be one of the coldest of the winter season. The runways and roads were clear; however, a blanket of snow still covered the grass. But the real challenge was the wind. From the moment you left the pilot lounge, the wind did its best war dance on your face. Frigid temperatures mixed with short gusts of wind made for the longest walk ever. He wanted to talk during the walk. I found myself exceptionally quiet. It wasn't that I was being standoffish with him. My mind simply couldn't think of anything else but how to escape this wind. It had found every possible opening it could in my outfit, sliding through gaps between my leather jacket and scarf, even punishing me for the slightest space between my socks and my thermals.

The wind. I came here to start my flying lessons, but little did I know the wind would ultimately be the real lesson of the day.

After finally making it to the hangar, I got the chance to get acquainted with the plane. It was an absolute beauty to me... a Piper Cherokee 140. A bit tight for my 6'4" build, but it was heaven nonetheless. As I saw it, this plane was the ticket to my goal of becoming a private pilot and a critical part of my ability to get into the sky and get closer to God (at least from the point of altitude). After what seemed like an eternity of walking around the plane, conducting an extensive inspection, we were ready for takeoff.

We got in the plane, seat belts locked, headsets on. With the engine roaring, we completed our "engine run up," one of the last series of tests before taking off.

Now my heart was racing. Adrenaline was pumping. Watching the instructor talk back and forth with ATIS and then shifting to Ground Control, I was literally losing my mind. All kinds of thoughts of those who have already journeyed this path before me crossed my mind: the Wright brothers, my childhood friend who became a pilot, the pilots who fly commercially and get us safely from one place to another, the farmer who flies his crop-duster across his field... they all are a part of the flight log of aviation history. And I was getting ready to join them.

I was jolted back into the situation at hand as my instructor informed me we were taking off on runway thirty-three. As we completed our taxi to the runway and turned to line ourselves up centerline, I noticed that the wind was blowing toward us with fierceness, double the strength of what I experienced during my walk to the hangar. This didn't make sense. *"Why are we flying into the wind? Isn't that counterproductive?"* I asked. My instructor replied confidently, *"We take off and land into the wind... always."*

Okay. Whatever.

Remember when I told you the wind would become a major part of this lesson? Well, now I was focused on the wind. Again. And now I was a bit confused and wondering if this guy knew what he was talking about. Because in my mind, my natural "limited pilot experience" mind, all I could comprehend was all the times we had ridiculous gusts of wind in Philadelphia and how people were pushed down the street by the wind. A plane should be no different. To take my theory further—leaning to my own unde standing —we always hear the old Irish blessing that goes:

May the road rise to meet you.
May the wind always be at your back.
May the sun shine warm upon your face.
May the rains fall soft upon your fields.
And until we meet again,
may the Lord hold you in the palm of His hand.

Did you see that part about the wind? It CLEARLY says "at your back," right? So as far as I was concerned… this dude had the plane faced in the wrong direction.

Well, we took off down the runway. The throttle was full and so was my spirit.My instructor began the pull on the yoke, and we were lifting up off the ground. Before I could even gather myself, I realized that we had climbed pretty quickly and cars were nothing but little moving blocks on the ground. By the gauge in front of me, I could see that we were almost 3,000 feet up in the sky!

As he handed the controls over to me, I began to get adjusted to the relationship between the plane and the wind. The lift and weight, the thrust and the drag… forces that made this all possible. I realized very quickly that the wind was to be respected and can be utilized to create optimal situations in flight.

After an hour or so, it was time to land. Again, we discussed briefly about the wind. My instructor assured me landing into the wind was a good thing. Still a little confused, but trusting his word, we began our approach at 1500 feet. I watched intently as he navigated the wind, talking with the tower the whole time. As the world slowly enlarged itself back to life-size proportions, I felt humbled, realizing that I had much to learn about the world in the clouds.

LEARN TO LOVE THE WIND.

After a soft landing and securing the plane, we walked back to the lounge. Yes, the wind was still blowing like crazy. Yes, the temperature was still frigid. Yes, it still found every open space in my outfit. But this time I wasn't so focused on the temperature or the open spaces. I was thinking about the relationship of the wind and my ability to fly.

I asked my instructor to explain again why we took off and landed into the wind. What he said next changed everything for me:

"We want to take off in the wind because we use the wind to create the lift needed to get the plane up in the sky," he said. "Sure, a commercial jet can use its huge engines to manipulate a few things, but single engine guys need every ounce of wind at our face when we take off. Makes the climb much easier. When we land, we need the wind at our face to help slow the plane down, or we come in too fast. The landing would be hard, and we could possibly run out of runway to stop."

Well, my life changed right there, because I realized that God was speaking to me at that very moment. This flight lesson was just as much about flying through life as it was about flying a plane.

See, in life we tend to run away from the winds of life… the winds of change. The winds of life come in many forms, sweeping in from many corners of our earth:

- People talking about us.
- Rocky relationships on our jobs and in our families.
- Challenges in the church.
- Naysayers who spread negativity over our field of dreams.
- Disobedient children.
- Fears that keep us from chasing our goals.
- Insecurities.
- The negativity we face even when we're introducing positive change to our lives and the lives of others.
- The disappointment of being the recipient of all of that negative energy.

You get the picture.

Oftentimes, we run from the wind of our lives. We want no part of the challenge of having a wind gust directly at our face. And why should we? It makes our walk down the street of life that much more difficult. It's easier to have wind at our back, to push us and aid us in getting away faster. At least we think. Here's what I learned about the wind… and life for that matter.

We cannot control the wind.

The wind can be manipulated, utilized, and harnessed, but we cannot create and control it. And before we get into a long scientific dialogue about wind creation and arguments about wind tunnels, etc., let me say this: You can create wind of your own. Look, you can even "break wind." But you cannot stop the winds that nature brings. The jet streams of air, the cold and warm fronts, the frigid temperatures that ride into our streets and cities on the flying carpet of wind… none of us can change that.

Life is the same way. The winds life brings are similar to that of Mother Nature's: They are unstoppable. They are coming. They are going to happen. There is no use trying to create winds. Learn to use the wind instead.

Stop walking into wind. Instead, take off!

Challenges in life are inevitable, unstoppable like the wind. You can't do anything about that. But you can choose how you utilize the wind to get to where you are going. Yes, wind in your face is a problem if you're walking—but perfect when you are preparing for taking off for flight! Many times the problem we face in our lives is because we find ourselves thinking about walking in it, not flying into it and through it. The change of mindset and method makes all the difference.

The wind is exactly what you need to get to the heights and destinations you desire.

You need the wind. Embrace it. Love it. Stop being so mad at the fact that it's there. Yes, they talk about you. Yes, it stings, just like the frigid wind on my walk to the hangar that day. However, that same wind I was so unhappy with—I love it now! Why? Because now I use it, manipulate it, to lift my plane into the sky and soar to my destination. Treat the winds of your life the same way. Turn your plane toward it, open up your throttle, and race your plane down the runway. Just a simple, almost effortless tug on the yoke will lift you and your life far above the nonsense you normally would have to walk though. God will not stop the challenges in your life, but He has given you the ability to use them and the wind that they create to soar and fly above.

Remember, the winds will always be there. So let's use them to our advantage. Stop walking; start flying.

CHAIN BREAKERS

Can you identify the "winds" in your life? What are they? Have you faced them or turned your back to them?

_____

_____

_____

_____

How can you utilize the "wind" in order to take flight?

_____

_____

_____

_____

Everyone that flies must have a destination in mind. You cannot simply fly around in the sky forever. So, what is your destination once you take flight? Where are you flying to?

_____

_____

_____

BREAKING THE CHAIN OF RUSHING THE TIMING OF SUCCESS

VIII

Let me start of by saying that I love just about every sport. I think becoming a polished, exceptionally trained athlete is one of the most amazing realities we can accomplish with our bodies. Of all the sports, I love baseball. It's my personal favorite. And honestly, it's not because of the huge home runs or the excitement of the World Series or even the base stealing or great glove plays... I love baseball because of the timing needed to be successful.

I know... you're wondering, *"What in the world is this guy taking about?"* All the excitement of baseball, all of the things he could have fallen in love with, and this guy says timing? *Timing?* I get it. So let me explain.

I've watched the greats for years, both pitchers and batters, and I am convinced that the batter's box and the pitching mound are the ultimate test of preparation, patience, and timing.

You have these huge athletes coming up to bat. They step into the box, many over six feet tall with muscular frames that tell of months of training. They dig their toes into the dirt and take a stance, their eyes with a warrior-like gaze, staring at the pitcher to detect any flaw in his delivery. They look at how many times he wipes his pitching hand against his jersey. Is he nervous? Is he trying to get enough grip to throw a heavy breaking ball? He keeps pacing the mound. Is he confused on what to pitch to me? Maybe he's just trying to wait me out and make me overly anxious. A myriad of thoughts runs through the batter's mind. But in the end, their only goal: to time that swing perfectly, marry the sweet spot of the bat with the seams of the ball, and make great contact.

The pitcher on the mound surveys the scene. Like Iron Man, he is reading all the data coming into his visual analysis system. Except his suit is not a metal one... It's a mental one. See, the stronger the pitcher's mental state is, the more effective he is, even in the most adverse situations. With an arsenal of pitches in his tool belt, he is gauging the batter's last performance, remembering the game tape, analyzing the batter's stance, watching his grip on the bat, accepting or rejecting his catcher's pitch suggestion, making a decision on pitch location and which pitch to throw, and executing this all in an average of ten to fifteen seconds.

And then the moment of decision comes.

The pitcher winds up and releases the ball, intent on realizing everything he imagined in his mind. He's sure that the batter believes another fastball is coming inside and away. He's analyzed the last five swings and believes the batter is too anxious. He thinks to himself, Even if this guy catches on to the fact that I'm throwing a breaking ball to the outside corner, he won't be able to act in time to adjust and get a good swing.

But the batter has something else in mind. He is content with hugging the plate even if it means getting hit. Partly ego—he refuses to be punked by a pitcher—but mostly because his favorite pitch to hit, the one he's most successful with, is a low, outside corner ball, the ones that cross the plate right at the height of his bent knee. He sees the pitch. He knows what it is a split second after it leaves the pitcher's hand. It's the one he loves. The one he's been knocking back to the warning track since he was a high school standout. This is the moment that he's been waiting for.

But believe it or not, this is the point where most mistakes happen. All the conditions are met. From everything that he can see, success is in his grasp. A definite home run. But realize, when everything is right is the exact moment everything can go wrong. He may swing too early; he may hit the ball late; he may produce a foul ball or a pop up. The key to a successful bat-ball marriage at this point is about timing.

Now some may give a rebuttal to this thought and claim that he can make contact early and still get on base. He can be a tad late and hit opposite field. All these things are slightly possible.

TIMING IS EVERYTHING.

As in life sometimes, even the mistake can work out. But we aren't talking about mistakes. We're talking about methods that we can consistently execute and reproduce constantly in our lives to be consistent in our life's ball-bat love connection. All of the batter's weight training and all of his cardio and all of his specialized batter motion exercises are great. I mean, really, you need those things in order to do wont things in that batter's box. But if you cannot hit the ball, if you cannot be patient and wait for your pitch, if your timing is off... none of your weight training matters. All your muscles, chiseled from the off season workouts, paired with your embroidered armbands and tight-fitting jersey, look absolutely great... resting comfortably on the bench after your strikeout.

Life is the same way. You can prepare for your next level. All the things you need can line up and be in place... your mentor, your protégé, your support group, your faith, your personal relationships, your family and finances... and still, without understanding timing and the perfected use thereof, you can find yourself sitting on life's bench, frustrated at your strikeout.

Here are some of the great life lessons from the batter's box:

Stop blaming others for your strikeout.

When you are in the batter's box, you have the control. If it's too much pressure on you at the time, you can back out of the box and call for time. You can change your stance to fit what's comfortable for you. You can stand at the top of the box or deep into the bottom of the box. You can stand on the far edges of the box or the inside edges. The point is... once you get set and the pitcher throws, it's all on you. You can't blame the pitcher; you can't blame the crowd. You can't blame the TV announcers; you can't blame your teammates. It's all on you.

So many times we find ourselves blaming others for what happens in our own batter's box of life. We find ourselves blaming the crowd for all of the missed pitches we swing at. We curse the umpire for calling the strikes and announcing that we struck out. Why? He didn't swing at the pitches... You did! Here's my favorite...

We blame the pitcher for throwing funny-moving pitches and throwing too fast and throwing pitches to knock us out of the box and then throwing across the plate to surprise us, throw off our timing, and strike us out. Well, what did you actually expect him to do? He plays for the other team! He's not your boy! And even if he is, in this scenario, he's wearing the other jersey. (Message!) Stop complaining about what pitches life is throwing your way. They may come a little fast, they may move across the plate, but stick in your batter's box and wait for your pitch.

Stop complaining about wild pitches.

I remember the infamous now-retired major league pitcher Mitch Williams. They called this guy the "Wild Thing" because, quite frankly, the more he stayed on the mound, the wilder his pitches got. It's also important to note that he looked the part too. His journey with the Rangers, Cubs, and Phillies was one of amazement. People loved to see him pitch, not because of his accuracy and mental ability to break down a batter. You wanted to see him pitch because his pitching motion would sometimes literally make him fall off the mound. And you came to see him because you were almost certain to see him hit someone, be it batter, umpire, or the back wall.

Cubs manager Don Zimmer said Williams *"did everything ninety-nine miles an hour,"* and teammate and close friend Mark Grace said, *"Mitch pitches like his hair's on fire."* The New Yorker baseball reviewer Roger Angell chortled over his *"scary, hilarious antics,"* saying, *"he flung the ball and then... flung himself after it, winding up with his back to home plate... peering over his left shoulder in case anyone accidentally made contact."* [2]

DON'T LEAVE THE BATTER'S BOX.

I bring him up (bless his soul) not to chide him for his performance, but to prove a point. The batters of the teams that Mitch faced all had something in common. What, you ask? They all made the conscious decision to get in the batter's box and face Mitch. So no matter what happened in that box, no matter what pitch was thrown, at their head or across the plate, they couldn't complain. But that wasn't the only thing. Because he threw so wildly, when he realized he wasn't getting a ball across the plate, he would start throwing basic pitches in order to reduce the chances of a wild pitch. Well, this would result in often times a great pitch for a well-prepared batter.

Game six of the 1993 World Series proves my point. This particular inning, after putting multiple people on base and his legendary erratic delivery beginning to fail him, Mitch gave up a walk-off home run to Joe Carter to lift the Toronto Blue Jays over the Philadelphia Phillies and deliver the trophy to Toronto.

I say all of that to say this:

Never complain about the wild pitches in your life. You may have to duck a few while you're in the batter's box, but just wait. Be patient. Most times, you will find that the one throwing the erratic pitches in your life now realizes that you aren't fazed anymore by the routine, and he will be forced to put something over the plate... a pitch you can really hit, a pitch that works for you, something that will allow you to go down in history for knocking it out of the park with a home run of your own.

Learn to love the game.

Life is a team sport. You may get to pick some of your teammates, but you don't get to pick the pitches that get thrown your way. Learn to love this reality, and it will make your time in the batter's box that much more enjoyable.

CHAIN BREAKERS

Have you allowed your strikeouts to become reasons to blame others? Was it really their fault or can you identify something that you could have done differently?

_____

_____

_____

_____

_____

Have you found your stance in the batter's box in your life? Do you know what "your pitch" looks like?

_____

_____

_____

_____

_____

_____

_____

Do you really love life or are you just here? Do you go into the batter's box of your life with a smile, or is it a chore to swing the bat?

_____

_____

_____

_____

_____

Based on your performance at the plate, would people pick you as a star player? If not, what can you do to change that?

_____

_____

_____

_____

_____

_____

_____

_____

_____

A Penny for Your Thoughts...

Here is a section for additional notes.
Write down what you are feeling, thinking, wondering...

_____

_____

_____

_____

_____

_____

_____

_____

_____

_____

_____

_____

_____

_____

_____

_____

_____

_____

_____

_____

_____

_____

FINAL THOUGHTS

IX

"Don't copy the behavior and customs of this world, but let God transform you into a new person by changing the way you think. Then you will learn to know God's will for you, which is good and pleasing and perfect." —Romans 12:2 (New Living Translation)

I love the New Living Translation version of that scripture. It delivers such a beautiful yet plain summary of the collective theme that I sought to present to you in this journey that we have shared through my experiences.

Life, and the way we are often told to think—often by media, peers, teachers, even molded at times by our countless reactions to experiences—sometimes finds us locked into patterns of thought that simply confine us and create chains that suppress our ability to approach the situation with the excellence of analysis that God has given all of us an opportunity to utilize.

As you can see through my words, stories, and thoughts, I am of sound mind and belief that the keys to our success, the breaking of the inner barriers and chains in your life, are mental first, long before you execute any action in the physical realm.

Learning to read God's directional signs in our lives; seeing things not just in a topical way, reading only the surface, but being able to dig deeper to find the lesson in it all not only helps us change our perspective, but allows us to see the road to success.

How do you see the directional signs of life? Not just through the general revelations that God provides in the wind and the trees, the majestic presentment of the moon and stars, but through special revelation... His specially written messages penned with you in mind. Learning God's written word is critical, because it was written not just for our knowledge of Him, but to help us realize the amazing things that He desires for our lives! Understanding who God is, and how He speaks in our lives, helps us to see with clarity beyond our circumstances, not as the victim, but the victor. And it is this train of thought that becomes so important when dealing with this life as we know it.

I pray always for your clarity on this journey in life; praying for spiritual eyes and ears to help you see and hear God through the daily messages brought to you on the shoulders of everyday occurances. Success is a blessing that God intends for us all to enjoy, without the burdensome chains we've been wearing for so long.

So let's lose the chains, break free, and live the way God intended us to live.

Until we meet again...

Malik

Final Notes

What key points did you discover along this journey that can help you as you go forward?

_____

_____

_____

_____

_____

_____

_____

Do you see some things in your life in a different way?
If so, what are they?

_____

_____

_____

_____

_____

_____

_____

_____

_____

FREEDOM CREED

Fill in the blanks of the creed with words from some of the passages found in the pages of this book.

Cut the creed out, place it on your desk.

Take it with you wherever you go.

Believe it, own it. It is not just words...it's who you truly are.

My name is _____.

I am of a chosen generation, a royalty priesthood; because I am a child of _____. I am blessed not because I live in my desires but because I live within my _____. God has given me _____ and _____ that make room for me wherever I go. Though I may have to walk through some dark places in this life, I will have no _____, because _____ is with me.

I am a leader, who leads by my _____ to others. This not only blesses others, but blesses myself. I know _____ I am, and _____ I am. The _____ in me is bigger than the problems around me.

I will _____ a young person because it is my _____, not an option. The _____ - _____ of a young person matters to me, even if they are not my child/family.

I believe in progress, and I will never get caught up staying in my _____. I believe in my vision and I will think in _____ and _____ in order to see it through.

I cannot control the _____ in my life, but I can utilize them to fly high above any obstacles I may face, and use them to arrive my destination and goal.

I am an All Star. I will not blame others for my _____, nor will I complain about _____ _____. I will stay in the batter's box until I hit a _____ _____. I have broken the _____ in my life. I am no longer bound. **I am free.**

References:

1. Jordan's Jumper Secures Chicago's Sixth Title
   http://www.nba.com/history/finals/19971998.html

2. Mitch Williams, Wikipedia
   http://en.wikipedia.org/wiki/Mitch_Williams

I'm proud of you.
I believe in you.

Malik

INDEX

A

Arsenio Hall...47

B

baseball...85

batter's box 87

changing lanes..................................66

C

Coming to America............................47

controlling the wind.........................81

defeating your fear...........................28

D

Dominican Republic..........................17

E

Eddie Murphy.....................................47

F

flying a plane.....................................77

following the guide...........................34

G

God given design........................20-21

great endings.....................................68

H

halted legacy building......................55

heights and destinations.................82

humble beginnings...........................68

I

Impactful leadership.........................41

K

knowing your value...........................49

M

Martin Luther King, Jr.............. 42, 55

mentorship...56

Michael Jordan..................................68

misunderstanding.............................39

Mitch Williams...................................88

Mortimer and Randolph....................50

O

obstacles......................................48,50

P

Philadelphia Phillies.................. 89-90

pitcher..85-86

poor thinking.....................................65

Psalms 23...33

R

road rage..66

Royal Priesthood...............................40

S

self-help books..................................55

sharks...25

spirit of service.................................42

spiritual energy.................................32

stages and steps...............................72

staying in your lane...........................66

stingrays..26-27

strikeout...87

T

taking off 77

timing of success..............................85

"tip off" moment................................70

To whom much is given,

much is required...............................41

W

who you are.................................. 39, 50

wild pitches.......................................88

wind..77

World Series.......................................85

Y

your gift..21

Find Malik online:

----

www.malikboyd.com

facebook.com/malikboyd
twitter.com/malikboyd
instagram.com/_malikboyd_

About the Author

Malik Boyd is the founder of *Malik Boyd Ministries* and *The 180 Movement*, a organization that works with Christian ministry leaders and youth groups to develop life-changing mentorship programs for youth, and other Christian based resources for empowering the next generation of Godly leaders. He currently serves as the Worship Champion at First African Baptist Church in Philadelphia, Pa. under the leadership of Pastor Terrence D. Griffith.

Active beyond the four walls of church, Malik created MENtors, a mentoring program for at risk male youth. To date, MENtors has been successful at pairing youth with qualified, and passionate mentors, educating youth on opportunities.

Malik is also the founder of Premiere Brand, LLC., a creative design firm in Philadelphia. With over a decade at the helm, he has led the creative team of Premiere through an impressive run, garnering national accolades, and charting a client list inclusive of Fortune 500, national, and regional clients.

As the President of the Philadelphia Young Democrats, Malik works to guide the organization's mission of ensuring the prosperity and vitality of young Philadelphians.

Malik is the proud father of two beautiful girls, Mikayla Jolie, and Diamond Amore. He has always believed in God's blessings through the family and the strength that it brings.

Other Titles by the Author:

Power Of One:
Perfecting Life One Post At A Time

·

www.ingramcontent.com/pod-product-compliance
Lightning Source LLC
Chambersburg PA
CBHW071010040426
42443CB00007B/747